JAANA WOODBURY

Prayers of a Prodigal

A DEVOTIONAL FOR THE LOST AND FOUND

Copyright ® 2025 by Jaana Woodbury
Published by UNITED HOUSE Publishing
All rights reserved. No portion of this book may be reproduced or shared in any form - electronic, printed, photocopied, recording, or by any information storage or retrieval system, without prior written permission from the publisher. The use of short quotations is permitted.

Scripture quotations are from the ESV® Bible (The Holy Bible, English Standard Version®), © 2001 by Crossway, a publishing ministry of Good News Publishers. ESV Text Edition: 2025. The ESV text may not be quoted in any publication made available to the public by a Creative Commons license. The ESV may not be translated in whole or in part into any other language. Used by permission. All rights reserved.

Scripture quotations taken from The Holy Bible, New International Version®, NIV®. Copyright © 1973, 1978, 1984, 2011 by Biblica, Inc. Used with permission of Zondervan. All rights reserved worldwide. www.zondervan.com

Scripture quotations taken from the (NASB®) New American Standard Bible®, Copyright © 1960, 1971, 1977, 1995, 2020 by The Lockman Foundation. Used by permission. All rights reserved. lockman.org

Scripture quotations marked TPT are from The Passion Translation®. Copyright © 2017, 2018, 2020 by Passion & Fire Ministries, Inc. Used by permission. All rights reserved. ThePassionTranslation.com.

ISBN - 978-1-952840-77-7

UNITED HOUSE Publishing Clarkston, Michigan
info@unitedhousepublishing.com www.unitedhousepublishing.com
Author Photograph: Kyle Munson
Interior Design: Talitha McGuinness;
talitha@unitedhousepublishing.com
Printed in the United States of America 2025 - First Edition

SPECIAL SALES:
Most UNITED HOUSE books are available at special quantity discounts when purchased in bulk by corporations, organizations, and special interest groups. For more information, please email orders@unitedhousepublishing.com.

DEDICATION

I dedicate this book to the love of my life, Sam.
Our story is my favorite.
Ofa atu, my love. My forever.

To our four beautiful daughters:
Salia, Kya, Fae, and Lovai

There aren't enough words to adequately express how much
we love you.
You are our pride and joy. Beautiful and blessed beyond measure.
Woodburys can do hard things!

CONTENTS

I - PREFACE 7

II - INTRODUCTION- FINDING OUR WAY BACK 9

III - PRODIGAL SON 13

Transforming Self-Reflection into Diving Perception

Angry - Peaceful 15

Anxious - Calm 19

Avoidant - Acceptant 21

Depressed - Desire to Live 23

Fearful - Courageous 27

Stressed - Surrendered 29

Prideful - Humble 31

Lustful - Pure 33

Judgment - Grace 37

Grief - Solace 39

Greed - Generosity 41

Resentment - Forgiveness 43

Distracted - Focused 45

Manipulative - Authentic 47

Impatient - Patient 49

Withdrawn - Engaged 51

6 / Prayers of a Prodigal

Dishonest - Honest 53

Impulsivity - Self-Control 57

Defeated - Victorious 61

Controlling - Letting Go 63

Rebellious - Obedient 67

Shameful - Virtuous 69

Destructive - Constructive 73

Stubborn - Flexible 75

Irresponsible - Responsible 79

Hopeless - Hopeful 81

Vindictive - Compassionate 83

Self-centered - Considerate 85

Idolatry - Truth 87

Doubt - Faith 91

IV - CONCLUSION - REMAINING 93

V - ACKNOWLEDGEMENTS 95

VI - RESOURCES 96

VII - ABOUT THE AUTHOR 99

PREFACE

I first met Jaana in seventh grade during a soccer match. Our introduction was brief and, since we attended different schools, I assumed that would be the extent of our connection. If you had told me back then, at twelve years old, I would marry her at twenty, welcome our first beautiful daughter at twenty-one while living in Japan as a Marine, and then find myself at twenty-four in my parents' house outside St. Louis for an intervention with friends and family in the living room, I would have thought you were telling a wild tale.

Yet, here we are 16 years of marriage later. By the grace of God, we are sober today, but our journey was not without its struggles. In the early days of our sobriety, we faced separation for nine long months. Uncertainty loomed and we weren't sure if our marriage would survive. The thought of having a broken family was a hard reality. However, at the request of our oldest daughter, we made the courageous decision to try to be a family again, and through reconciliation, we began to build a life where sobriety and faith became our cornerstones. In early sobriety, we welcomed our second daughter and continued celebrating sobriety milestones year after year. We also participated in a Sesame Street special covering addiction and mental health where our family was filmed for a documentary, eventually winning a Daytime Emmy. The turning point in our family's life was when we found our spiritual home in a nondenominational church and uncovered the truth we had long been searching for, getting baptized shortly after. After sixteen years of marriage and four daughters later, we felt God call us away from Southern California and settled in Tennessee, where we bought our first, forever home.

As I reflect on our journey, I am reminded of the words from James 1:2-4, ESV: "Count it all joy, my brothers, when you meet trials of various kinds, for you know that the testing of your faith produces steadfastness. And let steadfastness have its full effect, that you may be perfect and complete, lacking in nothing."

When I think of Jaana, I am continually reminded of Proverbs 31:10-12, ESV: "An excellent wife who can find? She is far more precious than jewels. The heart of her husband trusts in her, and he will have no lack of gain. She does him good, and not harm, all the days of her life."

This passage captures Jaana perfectly. A good wife is a gift from the Lord, and her diligence is not just for herself but also for me and our girls. I have truly been blessed by God to have found this in my wife. Through all her trials and tribulations, she has gained the endurance, strength, and perseverance needed to write this devotional and serve others. I pray her obedience to God's call on her life will inspire you through these words.

With love,
Samuel Woodbury

INTRODUCTION
Finding Your Way Back

PRODIGAL /'prädəgəl/ - a person who leaves home and behaves recklessly, but later makes a repentant return.

In my mid-twenties, I found myself praying a desperate prayer, the kind that only comes when your world is falling apart. My life had unraveled into a storm of addiction and depression, leaving me hollow and exhausted. The passion I once carried had faded to a faint ember, barely enough to keep me going. I was drowning—caught in a relentless cycle of chaos, helplessness, and overwhelming despair.

In that moment, I stood at a crossroads, faced with a choice I could no longer avoid. I could let the darkness take over, giving in to the weight of it all, or cling to the illusion that I had everything under control. Neither path felt certain, but I knew one thing: I couldn't keep living like this. Something had to change, and fast!

I was a prodigal, lost in denial, desperately trying to maintain the appearance of normalcy. Yet in that moment of brokenness, I finally cried out to God, ready to confront a difficult truth. *I could not fix this on my own.* My life had become unmanageable, and the connection with God that I thought was irreparably broken was the very thing I needed most. If you find yourself in a similar place, feeling hopeless or alone, know this: **you are not alone in your struggle.**

Brokenness is not something to be ashamed of. Life is filled with seasons of pain and loneliness, sometimes caused by our own choices and sometimes by circumstances beyond our control. These moments can feel overwhelming, as if they will last forever. The world often offers quick fixes, but they only deepen the chasm between us and God. They distract us, offering temporary relief while leaving the root of the pain untouched. It is often in the moments when we feel completely burned out that we begin to see how far we have really strayed.

At the same time, we contend with a spiritual enemy who thrives on our isolation. He whispers lies of defeat, convincing us that change is impossible and we are too far gone. He wants us to remain trapped in shame and hopelessness, far from the freedom God desires for us. But the truth is, even in our darkest moments, God's light breaks through. He promises freedom, healing, and hope to those who turn to Him. He sees you, even when you feel invisible, and His love remains constant. God is never finished with us. He enters the very mess we hoped no one would see—and rewrites redemption over the places we thought were beyond repair.

Surrendering to God isn't about giving up—it's about leaning into the strength to begin again. If you're questioning whether restoration is possible, hear this: it is. The darkest seasons don't last forever. On the other side is a deeper, more beautiful story only He can write. God is the Master of redemption. He takes what was meant for harm and transforms it for good. In His hands, nothing is wasted—not even the parts you wish you could erase.

Over the next thirty days, we will explore the beliefs and behaviors that hinder us from growing and embracing the identity God has lovingly designed for us. As you reflect, you will discover you are so much more than your circumstances. Like the father in the parable of the prodigal son, God is patiently waiting for you to come home. No distance is too far, and no mistake is too great. As long as you have breath, there is hope. You were created for a purpose, and I invite you to approach this devotional with an open heart, even if your faith feels shaky right now. God does not require perfection—just a willingness to seek Him.

Each day of this devotional is built on four key elements: a reflection, a petition, a gratitude statement, and a prayer for others. Prayer is a powerful weapon in spiritual warfare, capable of tearing down strongholds and renewing our minds. Gratitude shifts our perspective, reminding us of God's faithfulness and goodness even in the hardest times. Praying for others draws us out of isolation, building the community that is so vital to healing and growth. Together, these elements create a rhythm of reflection and connection with God that will encourage and strengthen you.

My hope is that this devotional will lift your spirit and help you release the burdens weighing you down. You are not defined by your struggles or your past. We serve a God whose goodness knows no limits, a God who longs to restore and empower you to live righteously. I am no different from you. If it weren't for those who walked this path before me, offering their encouragement and prayers, I might not be here today. Their words and faith were a lifeline, reminding me of the hope I had nearly forgotten. So take these words to heart, hold onto your faith, and know this. You are not alone and never too far gone. You are loved and chosen.

In Christ,
A Prodigal

PRODIGAL SON

"The prodigal son in the Bible is a parable told by Jesus Christ to illustrate God's joy in welcoming a repentant sinner. The story concerns a man who divided his estate between his two sons. The younger son sold his share, left home, and spent his money on dissolute living. He returned home repentant. His father welcomed him with compassion and forgiveness, celebrating by having a feast. The elder son complained that his life of virtue and hard work had never been rewarded. The outraged self-righteousness of the elder son provides a marked contrast with the genuine humility of the younger. The story is told in Luke 15:11-32."

Standard Education Corporation (2006). New Standard Encyclopedia (Volume 13. p. 288)

DAY ONE
Angry to Peaceful

Do not repay evil with evil or insult with insult. On the contrary, repay evil with blessing, because to this you were called so that you may inherit a blessing.
1 Peter 3:9, NIV

Anger can often catch us off guard, rising up before we take the time to acknowledge God as the ultimate Judge. It shows up when we feel wronged, frustrated, or powerless, leaving us unsettled and tempted to take control. For many of us, anger feels like a natural response and something we're justified in holding on to. But in the end, it often leaves us feeling more broken than whole.

It's important to recognize that resolving anger isn't about fixing the people or circumstances around us. It is about surrendering our hearts to God and trusting Him with what feels unjust. James 1:19-20 (NIV) challenges us: "My dear brothers and sisters, take note of this: Everyone should be quick to listen, slow to speak and slow to become angry, because human anger does not produce the righteousness that God desires." These verses remind us that no matter how justified our anger feels, it cannot bring the peace or justice that only God can provide.

When anger wells up, we can pause and bring it to God in prayer. Psalm 37:8 (NIV) encourages us: "Refrain from anger and turn from wrath; do not fret—it leads only to evil." In these moments of prayer, we open ourselves to God's calming presence, allowing Him to realign our perspective. Though it is not always easy, each time we choose to seek His wisdom before reacting, we take a step toward reflecting His grace rather than our frustration.

Romans 12:19 (NIV) reminds us, "Do not take revenge, my dear friends, but leave room for God's wrath, for it is written: 'It is mine to avenge; I will repay,' says the Lord." These words free us from the burden of carrying every offense.

> **We don't have to fight for justice in our own strength because we serve a God whose justice is perfect.**

Instead, we can focus on reflecting His love and grace, even when it feels undeserved.

As we surrender our anger to God, we begin to experience His peace. We find it is not about denying our emotions but about letting Him transform them into opportunities for growth. Each time we respond with His love instead of reacting out of our frustration, we reflect His character in a world that desperately needs to see His grace. Together, we can trust God to work in and through our anger, bringing freedom, healing, and peace.

PETITION:

God, I understand that I am not defined by my unresolved anger. Guide me into a posture that allows me to identify any underlying issue that has potentially caused pain, resulting in a hardened heart. Bring aid so I may be able to experience peace and rid myself of any bitterness, rage, anger, brawling, and slander, along with any form of malice (Ephesians 4:31-32, NIV). Rather than act out of anger when I am hurt or offended, help me abide in Your instruction to live at peace.

GRATITUDE:

I am grateful for my ability to engage in healthy dialogue with others, regardless of any anger I may feel. I'm grateful for my ability to be made new in the attitude of my mind. I'm grateful for the guidance God gives and that He is an everlasting rock.

INTERCESSION:

Lord, we lift up every person burdened by anger and conflict. We ask that You bring them the clarity to see the root of their struggles and the courage to release them into Your hands. May Your peace, which transcends all understanding, guard their hearts and minds in Christ Jesus. Teach them to sow seeds of love, to extend grace where it is needed, and to walk in the freedom of forgiveness. Let Your favor rest upon them, bringing a peace that lasts not just for today, but for a lifetime.

AMEN

James 1:20; Psalm 37:8; Proverbs 15:18

DAY TWO
Anxious to Calm

Cast all your anxiety on him because he cares for you.
1 Peter 5:7, NIV

Coping with anxiety is no easy task. Anxiety is a deeply visceral response to nervousness, often overwhelming us and clouding our sense of peace. Successfully managing it requires intentional effort to remain grounded and in tune with God's truth and the world around us. Before we began our journey of healing, we often found ourselves trapped in unfavorable circumstances, letting our struggles dictate how we felt and responded. Anxiety thrives on worry and stress, leaving us vulnerable to spiritual attacks and disconnected from the peace God offers. What makes it even more challenging is that the things we feel anxious about are often outside of our control.

As we grow in our understanding of God's truth, we begin to recognize the spiritual nature of anxiety. There is an enemy who wants nothing more than for us to feel stuck, paralyzed by our anxious thoughts. It becomes clear that our earthly existence can place us in an unprotected state if we do not remain close to God.

{ **Staying anchored in Him is not just a comfort. It is a necessity.** }

God's Word speaks directly to our anxious hearts. In Matthew 6:34 (NIV), Jesus tells us, "Therefore do not worry about tomorrow, for tomorrow will worry about itself. Each day has enough trouble of its own." This verse is an invitation to release our daily struggles into God's hands and trust in His provision. It reminds us that we do not have to remain in the stormy waters of our anxious thoughts. Instead, we are invited into the calming oasis of God's presence, where His truth irrigates the barren places of our hearts and minds, bringing peace and restoration.

By staying connected to God and leaning into His promises, we can begin to overcome anxiety. It does not mean the challenges disappear, but it does mean we are no longer walking through them alone. God equips us with the strength to rise above the turmoil and embrace the peace that comes from trusting Him fully.

PETITION:

God, I understand You are above all things, and my anxieties are not mine to carry. Bring aid so I can learn to rely on you for feeling calm amid any anxious thoughts. Guide me into Your loving arms so I will be shielded against any anxieties that feel too burdensome to carry. I pray to always remember that when I choose to keep my eyes on You, I am surrendering to dwell in Your perfect peace.

GRATITUDE:

I am grateful God grants peace to troubled hearts. I am grateful to have a developing understanding that my anxieties aren't mine to carry alone, and that God renews hope. I am grateful I can offer my worries to God in prayer and trust Him in every situation.

INTERCESSION:

Lord, I come before You on behalf of those burdened by anxiety, asking for Your perfect peace to calm their hearts and minds. Let them experience the truth of Philippians 4:6-7, where You promise that as we bring our requests to You, Your peace will guard our hearts and minds. Strengthen them to stand firm, wearing the full armor of God, able to extinguish every flaming arrow of doubt and fear. Replace their anxious thoughts with the assurance of Your love and the promise of Your presence. We trust You to bring calm where there is chaos and strength where there is weakness.

AMEN

Philippians 4:6; Matthew 6:25; Psalm 94:19

DAY THREE
Avoidant to Acceptant

What, then, shall we say in response to these things? If God is for us, who can be against us?
Romans 8:31, NIV

Avoidant behaviors often serve as unhealthy coping mechanisms. When we find ourselves dodging people or situations, we're typically attempting to escape or distract ourselves from uncomfortable feelings. Throughout our lives, we may have faced challenges that left us feeling disappointed or misunderstood. Instead of confronting these disruptions head-on, we may fall into the unconscious habit of dismissing our uncomfortable emotions, believing avoidance will ultimately protect us. However, such behaviors can render us socially inept, hindering our ability to engage in fulfilling relationships.

One of the first steps toward building meaningful connections is recognizing our patterns of avoidance. When we learn to trust God with our lives, we begin to understand that every experience can be used for good. Over time, we can transform circumstances that once threatened to destroy us into catalysts for change, not only for ourselves but also for others. By embracing our testimony, we can overcome the barriers that previously kept us from cultivating a spirit of acceptance.

Practicing acceptance enables us to acknowledge our emotions and experiences without judgment, fostering resilience and clarity as we move forward. This step is crucial; to chart a new course, we first need to understand where we stand. Think of it like navigating with a map: it's nearly impossible to find your destination if you don't know your starting point.

> **Acceptance is a transformative skill that allows us to see clearly that God is sovereign and holds every detail of our lives in His hands (Psalm 37:23-25, NLT).**

Embracing acceptance doesn't mean we agree with every experience from our past; rather, it involves recognizing them as integral parts of our earthly journey without the impulse to avoid or alter them. With this certainty, we can rely on God to renew a steadfast spirit within us.

PETITION:

Lord, help me in the discovery of learning how to change my outlook on situations that I have been avoiding due to my own discomfort. Bring aid in letting go of expectations of myself and others that limit me from being able to adopt lessons that can be used to build my character. Guide me as I learn to accept life on Your terms and omit any reason to remain avoidant.

GRATITUDE:

I am grateful for the courage to accept circumstances that have been problematic. I am grateful to have the willingness to embrace the serenity God provides by moving into a place of acceptance. I am grateful to have the ability to accept people, places, and things exactly for what they are at this moment in time.

INTERCESSION:

I pray others can discover the true liberation found in God. May they gain insight into any avoidant behaviors keeping them disconnected from fully experiencing life. Help them to recognize these patterns and find the courage to confront them, allowing them to embrace the abundant life You have promised. Lord, guide them in breaking free from fear and hesitation, enabling them to engage more fully with themselves and others. May they understand that true freedom comes from surrendering to Your will and trusting in Your plan for their lives.

AMEN

Galatians 5:1; 1 Timothy 1:15; Psalm 19:14

DAY FOUR
Depressed to Desire to Live

The Lord is close to the brokenhearted and saves those who are crushed in spirit.
Psalm 34:18, NIV

Many of us encounter seasons in life where our enthusiasm for daily activities dwindles, leaving us feeling adrift and disengaged. This decline often occurs not because of any conscious choice, but due to an insidious shift in our thoughts that can trap us in a downward spiral. As we grapple with feelings of inadequacy, we may begin to isolate ourselves, creating barriers that prevent us from connecting with others. Over time, these feelings can coalesce into a negative belief system that distorts our self-image, causing us to forget our inherent worth and resigning us to a mindset of hopelessness.

Opening up about depression is no easy task, yet it is a crucial step toward acknowledging that we are not alone in our struggles. It can serve as a lifeline, reminding us that even in our weakest moments, when we feel most unworthy, we are seen and loved by a God who embraces us in our entirety. Although we may find ourselves far from where we want to be, we can still nurture a desire to move forward, rooted in the understanding that we are created beautifully in God's design.

Instead of focusing solely on the distance we have yet to traverse, we can also take time to reflect on the many challenges we have already faced and overcome.

{ **Each hardship endured adds to our resilience and shapes our journey.** }

By the grace of God, we can be freed from the chains of damaging thoughts and emerge with a renewed spirit, capable of seeing the world through a lens of hope.

We are reminded in Ephesians 3:20 that God is able to do immeasurably more than we could ever ask or imagine. This promise invites us to trust in His limitless power and ability to transform our lives, guiding us from despair to a place of healing and purpose.

PETITION:

Lord, help me to identify the reasons I have for living as a child of God. Bring aid through the promises of Your Word and give me the courage to embrace positive thoughts and truth. Guide me as I strive to overcome beliefs that no longer serve me and help me remain steadfast in the joys of life. I pray I am empowered to seek refuge in You and for complete understanding to combat any spirit of confusion. Give me eyes to see my life and myself through Your lens.

GRATITUDE:

I am deeply grateful for the ability to reach out to others and express my needs. It is a reminder of the importance of connection and vulnerability, both with God and the people He places in my life. I am thankful for the reassurance that I am never alone, even in moments of struggle or uncertainty. Knowing I can lean on God for strength and trust in the support of my community gives me peace and courage. It's a beautiful gift to experience His love through the encouragement and care of others, and I am reminded of His faithfulness every time I choose to reach out.

INTERCESSION:

I pray for those who are feeling down and struggling with depression. May they find the light that pierces through the darkness, reminding them that they are never alone. Help them to recognize that there is a loving God who seeks to bring joy and healing into every aspect of their lives. May they experience the warmth of His presence and the comfort of His love, guiding them toward hope and renewal. Surround them with support and encouragement, and instill in them the belief that brighter days are ahead.

AMEN

Psalm 6:9; Psalm 25:17; Romans 15:13

DEPRESSION DISCLAIMER:
If you are in crisis or having suicidal thoughts,
call 1-800-273-TALK (8255).

DAY FIVE
Fearful to Courageous

For God gave us a spirit not of fear but of power and love and self-control.
2 Timothy 1:7, ESV

You may have come across the quote by Jay Shetty: "When the fear of staying the same outweighs the fear of change, that is when we change." While this sounds like a reasonable plan for action, the reality of starting the process can feel overwhelming. Fear can be paralyzing, often rooted in feelings of inadequacy and powerlessness. It can convince us we lack the capability to overcome obstacles, leading us to settle into a state of indifference or perceived failure. Eventually, we are faced with a critical choice: Is fear worth sacrificing our overall well-being? In our standstill, we may grow weary of living in fear, and if this resonates with you, it may be time to take a step back and see fear for what it truly is: dominant, consuming, and in control of our actions.

> **When we begin to understand who God says we are, we realize the spirit of fear contradicts His desire for us to live with freedom and courage.**

With a willingness to change, we can start taking small steps of faith and find the strength to confront our fears. As we lean into God's strength, we come to understand that we were never meant to navigate our challenges alone. By reaching out and developing a sense of community, we discover hope in the knowledge that others have faced similar struggles. From my own experience, community has been a vital component of healing and growth; fear often fosters isolation, delaying meaningful connection.

Over time, as we build this supportive community, we cultivate a desire to stay connected. Together, we are reminded that we were created to embody a spirit of courage. With each step forward, we strive to navigate life with clarity and focus, overcoming the barriers that have kept us from fulfilling our purpose.

PETITION:

Lord, help me to come before You and lay my fears at Your feet. Guide me and remind me that I am bigger than my fears. Bring aid in helping me understand that through Your strength, I have the power to overcome my fears and insufficiencies. I pray to know the truth I have in You and the courage to dismiss any negative thoughts that are rooted in fear. I pray for the willingness to remain steadfast in truth and to believe You are greater than any earthly circumstance.

GRATITUDE:

I am grateful for courage and God's will for my life. I am grateful for my ability to bring my fears to God and trust the plans for my life are good. I believe I am courageous and that God will sustain truth amid any fear.

INTERCESSION:

Lord, I lift up those who may be feeling consumed by a spirit of fear. Remind them that You have not given us a spirit of fear, but of power, love, and a sound mind, as Your Word promises in 2 Timothy 1:7 (KJV). Surround them with Your protection and guard their hearts and minds against any fearful thoughts that try to take hold. Give them the courage to stand tall, clothed in Your strength, and to resist any scheme that challenges their ability to remain steadfast in You. May they feel Your peace that transcends understanding and be reminded of Your constant presence with them.

AMEN

Psalm 56:3; Isaiah 41:10; Joshua 1:9

DAY SIX
Stressed to Surrendered

Come to me, all you who are weary and burdened, and I will give you rest.
Matthew 11:28, NIV

Many of us intimately understand the sensation of tightness in our chests and shoulders that arises in moments of emotional tension. The burdens of hardship and emotional stress are universal experiences, inevitable in the ebb and flow of life. We encounter various triggers—demanding work environments, financial instability, and challenging relationships, all of which can intensify this stress. Often, we find ourselves feeling overwhelmed by the daily demands of life, leading us to seek refuge in behaviors that distract us from confronting our realities on God's terms. Unfortunately, these distractions can be both ineffective and harmful, leading us further from the peace we seek.

Through honest introspection, we can begin to recognize how many of our stress-induced behaviors are self-inflicted, masking the deeper issues that weigh us down. As we learn to lean into God's embrace, we can turn to Him in prayer and petition, making our needs known with a heart of gratitude (Philippians 4:6-7, NIV).

> **Through prayer, we trust that God will not only accompany us on our journey but will also meet us in our most pressing moments of need.**

When we earnestly seek to know God, the stressors of life can transform into doorways leading us toward impactful change. God beckons us to lay our burdens at His feet and to trust in His sovereignty over every aspect of our lives. In times of discouragement amid life's pressures, we have the power to take our thoughts captive

(2 Corinthians 10:5, ESV) and consciously choose to believe in God's promises. His divine design invites us to find comfort in Him, regardless of our circumstances. He offers us a peace that transcends all understanding (Philippians 4:7, ESV), but this peace requires us to relinquish control and place our faith in Him.

Faith serves as a powerful buffer against the stress that threatens to overwhelm us, equipping us with the unshakeable truth of God's Word. With God as our steadfast partner, we come to realize the desire to control our circumstances is often counterproductive. Instead, we have the choice to define our reality through the lens of God's truth, which invites us to transcend our limitations and embrace a deeper understanding of hope and healing.

PETITION:

Lord, help me grasp that I am not meant to bear my stress alone. Teach me to trust in Your sovereignty and recognize You are present in every detail of my life, even when it feels overwhelming. I pray for an unwavering belief in Your promise that You work all things together for good. Help me to surrender my stress and burdens into Your capable hands, knowing that You care for me deeply. May I find peace in the knowledge that I can rely on You, and may Your comfort fill my heart as I let go of the weight I carry.

GRATITUDE:

I am grateful I am created in the image of God (Genesis 1:26, NIV). I am grateful for the restoring power I have access to because of my ability to understand what I can and cannot control. I believe I am destined to live a life where I can relax in God's Will and trust that any stressors I have are temporary.

INTERCESSION:

I pray for others to experience the relaxing presence of God. I pray they develop an ability to healthfully navigate how to discern what they can and cannot control. I pray they can find the courage to lay it down before God and find a renewed spirit of hope.

AMEN

John 16:33; John 14:27; Lamentations 3:40

DAY SEVEN
Prideful to Humble

Humble yourselves before the Lord, and He will exalt you.
James 4:10, ESV

Viewing life through a prideful lens can obstruct our relationships and distance us from God. When pride takes root in our hearts, it can manifest as grandiosity, blinding us to the needs of others and diminishing our capacity for genuine connection. In this self-absorbed state, we may begin to demand more than our fair share from life, unwittingly stripping away our ability to engage in self-reflection and personal growth. While it's natural to take pride in our accomplishments, unchecked pride can inflate our sense of self-worth, blinding us to our true place within the larger fabric of humanity.

This overemphasis on self not only hampers our spiritual growth but also quenches the transformative power of the Holy Spirit within us. When we are preoccupied with our own agendas, we risk becoming ineffective in our communities, undermining our pursuit of righteous living. In stark contrast, the key to flourishing spiritually and deepening our relationship with God lies in the practice of humility.

> **Humility invites us to see ourselves as we truly are, not diminished, but as individuals intricately connected within God's creation, each with a unique role and purpose.**

It expands our focus from our own desires to the well-being of others, nurturing a compassionate spirit that fosters meaningful connections. As we embody humility in our daily lives, we cultivate a gentle strength that empowers us to serve those around us, enriching our spiritual journey and deepening our connection with God.

Living with a "right-sized" perspective allows us to recognize our dependence on divine grace, opening our hearts to the possibility of transformation. In this posture of humility, we can surrender our inflated egos and invite God to work through us as we navigate the complexities of life. As we embrace this journey, we discover that true freedom comes not from exalting ourselves, but from nurturing deeper relationships with God and those around us.

Ultimately, humility is not just an attitude but a transformative way of being that opens the door to a more authentic life. By walking this path, we uncover the beauty of connection and the deep joy of living in love, service, and grace.

PETITION:

God, help me to live with humility in my heart. Teach me to recognize that excessive pride can create a barrier between You and me. I pray for the insight to see how my pride has led me astray and the willingness to embrace humility so I can foster harmony in my relationships with others. May I find joy and fulfillment in living a humble life, understanding true strength lies in serving others and acknowledging my need for You. Guide me to delight in the beauty of humility, drawing closer to You and to those around me.

GRATITUDE:

I am grateful for the willingness to humble myself before God. I am grateful God exalts those who can set aside pride and invites me to rid all selfish desires. I am grateful for a sharpened sense of reality and my newfound freedom in self-awareness.

INTERCESSION:

I pray others can develop a sense of awareness that allows them to live in freedom from self. I pray they have a healthy sense of pride and can look to their peers with compassion and understanding. I pray they live with humility and feel closer to God as a result.

AMEN

Psalm 149:4; Proverbs 11:2; Luke 14:11

DAY EIGHT
Lustful to Pure

For everything in the world—the lust of the flesh, the lust of the eyes, and the pride of life— comes not from the Father but from the world.
1 John 2:16, NIV

Lust is a powerful internal force that can easily eclipse our rational thought and moral discernment. It manifests as an overwhelming yearning—whether for sexual gratification, power, material wealth, or the allure of excess. This intense desire often distorts our perception, leading us down a path that diminishes our ability to cultivate genuine intimacy and connection. At its essence, lust is transient and self-serving; it seeks immediate gratification without regard for the deeper emotional and spiritual consequences. When we surrender to lust, we not only inflict harm upon ourselves but also cloud our understanding of what true love and intimacy entail. Over time, this habitual indulgence can dull our sensitivity to virtue, making it increasingly difficult to discern what is pure and right. As a result, we limit the fullness of God's transformative work in our lives, obscuring the divine image we were created to reflect.

Conversely, purity represents a state of freedom from the shackles of desire that seek to enslave us and freedom from the chaos of a life driven by fleeting passions. Purity is both a gift from God and a divine mandate; it invites us to live in a manner that fosters joy, peace, and security. However, the pursuit of purity is not without its challenges. It requires unwavering commitment, discernment, and the courage to resist the seductive pull of worldly desires. This battle for purity is not merely a struggle against external temptations; it is a transformative journey that cultivates the strength to choose what aligns with God's will over what is simply gratifying in the moment.

Embracing a life of purity is not about restriction; rather, it is about liberation. It calls us to protect our hearts and minds, recognizing that our lives are meant for a higher purpose. A purpose that transcends self-satisfaction and the fleeting approval of others. When we commit ourselves to living purely, we create space for clarity in our lives and deepen our relationship with God, experiencing a sense of fulfillment and purpose.

> **To grasp the true freedom God intends for us, we must be willing to embrace a holistic approach to purity that permeates every aspect of our existence, from our thoughts and intentions to our actions and interactions with others.**

Purity is not an isolated endeavor but a way of being that reflects our desire to align with the heart of God.

The journey toward purity leads us to a place of authentic fulfillment and wholeness, where we can thrive in our identity as beloved children of God. In our pursuit, we discover that true joy is not found in the fleeting pleasures of lust but in the enduring love and grace that come from living a life devoted to righteousness. As we surrender to this higher calling, we become vessels of God's light, illuminating the world around us and inviting others into the transformative power of His love.

PETITION:

Lord, release me from any strong desires that lead to temptation. Grant me the gift of self-control and help me submit any lustful thoughts or ideas into Your care. Guide me toward wholesome activities and uplifting thoughts that reflect the transformation I seek in my life. Strengthen my resolve to focus on what is good, pure, and true, and help me cultivate a heart that longs for You above all else. May I find joy in aligning my thoughts and actions with Your will, and may Your presence guide me in every step I take.

GRATITUDE:

I am grateful I can look to God to gratify my desires. I am grateful for a solution that affords me freedom from indulging in activities that do not serve my higher purpose. I am grateful for the freedom from being overpowered by earthly lusts.

INTERCESSION:

I pray that others can discern the difference between lust and what is pure. May they recognize that lustful desires can never truly satisfy their hearts. I pray they will look to God to fill any voids they feel and find fulfillment in His love and purpose. Help them understand that giving in to lust is a misuse of their free will, and guide them toward a path of righteousness that honors their true selves. May they seek God's strength and wisdom to resist temptation and embrace the abundant life He offers.

AMEN

1 Peter 4:3; Galatians 5:16-21; 1 Timothy 2:22

DAY NINE
Judgment to Grace

Do to others as you would have them do to you.
Luke 6:31, NIV

Judging others is an instinctive cognitive process shaped by our personal biases and life experiences. While discernment is essential for making everyday choices, like what to wear or what to eat, being judgmental goes beyond this necessity and often leads to harmful conclusions about others. Our tendency to judge can fluctuate based on our spiritual health and emotional state; when we project our inner turmoil onto others, our judgment can become pervasive.

A quickness to judge often arises from feelings of inadequacy, fear, or jealousy. When we examine our judgments closely, we find that they are often byproducts of an ego under threat or unrealistic expectations. This distorted perspective leads us to operate from a skewed sense of reality, reflecting the negativity we direct toward others back onto ourselves. Consequently, dissatisfaction sets in, sabotaging our peace and happiness.

The antidote to judgment is grace. We should try to see others as God sees us. This requires intentional efforts and a capacity for compassion and understanding. Recognizing everyone is doing their best with the knowledge they possess allows us to release our judgmental tendencies and cultivate an attitude of grace. God desires for us to strengthen our capacity for grace, but to extend it to others, we must first learn to offer it to ourselves.

> As we deepen our relationship with God, we come to understand every good thing that flows through us is a reflection of His grace.

Through this grace, we find empowerment and develop genuine concern for the welfare of others. In this transformative journey, we discover a path to healing, unveiling God's unconditional love and acceptance.

PETITION:

Lord, help me see others through Your eyes, embracing the unique value and purpose each person holds. Teach me to set aside judgment and approach others with grace, even when it feels undeserved. May I extend the same grace to myself, recognizing my own imperfections while striving for growth. Strengthen my ability to remain objective, allowing Your love and compassion to guide my thoughts and actions. Help me foster understanding and empathy in my interactions, reflecting Your heart in all that I do.

GRATITUDE:

I am grateful for the desire to treat others as I want to be treated (Luke 6:31, AMP). I am grateful I can pause before I form any opinion and be fair in my interactions. I am grateful for God's grace and the chance to extend grace.

INTERCESSION:

I pray others remain mindful of their thoughts, especially those that lead to judgment. May they have the awareness to recognize these thoughts and opinions for what they truly are, allowing them to pause and reflect before acting on preconceived notions. Grant them the discernment to choose understanding over judgment and the courage to embrace empathy and compassion. Help them cultivate a mindset that seeks to understand others, fostering a spirit of unity and love in their interactions.

AMEN

Matthew 7:1; Romans 14:10; Matthew 7:2-5

DAY TEN
Grief to Solace

The Lord Himself goes before you and will be with you; He will never leave you nor forsake you. Do not be afraid; do not be discouraged.
Deuteronomy 31:8, NIV

Grief emerges when our assumptive world shatters, leaving us to navigate an uncharted and complex landscape. The loss of a loved one or something significant ignites a whirlwind of emotions, making any sense of normalcy feel impossibly distant. For many, grief is not a linear experience; instead, it manifests as an immediate surge of stress that disrupts our overall well-being. The emotional turmoil often takes us by surprise, leading us to question how such loss fits into God's design for our lives. As we begin to navigate this tumultuous journey, we eventually arrive at a crucial crossroads, where we must consciously choose to heal and move forward.

Over time, we discover that life after loss is not about piecing together what once was, but rather embracing the imperfections that remain. We come to understand that a constant reliance on God is essential as we adapt to our new reality and lean on the support of others. By focusing on nurturing our relationship with God, we find encouragement in our healing process. When we bring forth our pain and anguish, we can trust that He sees us, offering sufficiency for the deepest longings of our souls and relief from our sorrows.

In our moments of vulnerability, we begin to recognize the uniqueness of our experiences.

{ **God knows us intimately and serves as our one true comforter.** }

Amid grief and loss, we can regain our footing by resting in the assurance of His promises. Indeed, we can hold fast to the truth that God works all things together for good (Romans 8:28, ESV), guiding us gently through our darkest hours.

PETITION:

Lord, help me to find solace in my grief. Help me believe everything in Your plan is used for good, and I will find the strength to have hope. Help me navigate the unknown while resting in the truth of Your foreknowledge and predestined purpose for my life, regardless of any trials I may face.

GRATITUDE:

I am deeply grateful for God's sovereignty and the way His handiwork weaves through every detail of my life, even in ways I may not immediately see or understand. I am thankful that I can place my full trust in God's master plan, knowing that He is always working for good, even when circumstances feel uncertain or challenging. God's faithfulness reminds me that I don't need to have all the answers because He holds the ultimate purpose for my life in His hands.

INTERCESSION:

I pray others find comfort that can only come from God. I pray they learn to lean on God and their communities for support, knowing they aren't alone in their grief. I pray that their pain is not wasted but instead transformed into purpose, that they find meaning in their trials and use their stories for the glory of God. May they see how their brokenness can be redeemed into something beautiful, bringing hope and healing to others while deepening their own faith in the process.

AMEN

Psalm 34:1; Ecclesiastes 7:2-4; Matthew 5:4

DAY ELEVEN
Greed to Generosity

No one can serve two masters. Either you will hate the one and love the other,
or you will be devoted to one and despise the other.
You cannot serve both God and money.
Matthew 6:24, NIV

The line between ambition and greed can easily become blurred. Throughout history, greed has been perceived as a destructive force, playing a significant role in the decline of once-flourishing nations. This insatiable desire is not easily defined; what one person may consider excessive might appear entirely justifiable to another. While we often associate greed with the relentless pursuit of wealth, it can also reveal itself as self-centered behavior and a chronic dissatisfaction with life. Greed stands in direct opposition to a life rooted in God's teachings, creating a cycle of endless discontent.

When we allow greed to dictate our lives, we find ourselves entangled in a web of self-interest, adopting the troubling belief that enough is never truly enough. This relentless pursuit fosters maladaptive behaviors that lead to internal chaos and strain our relationships with others.

As we seek to live more healthily, we must critically evaluate our connections with people, places, and possessions. We may come to realize that we have assigned undue value to external achievements and material possessions, often sacrificing our well-being in the quest for more. While enjoying abundance is not inherently wrong, God calls us to be diligent stewards of what we possess, emphasizing the condition of our hearts over our material wealth.

Inviting a generous God into our lives unveils the transformative freedom found in selfless giving.

> **Living generously means releasing the expectation of reciprocation, trusting that God will provide for all our needs.**

We begin to recognize that a noble purpose in this life is enriching the lives of those around us. By liberating ourselves from the clutches of greed, we create space to flourish within God's divine economy, discovering the joy, lasting impact, and spiritual fulfillment that come with a life devoted to generosity.

PETITION:

Lord, help me identify where there may be greed in my life. Help me understand that greed is a selfish desire and not what You intended for me. Help me establish willful generosity and cultivate my heart to steward Your gifts accordingly.

GRATITUDE:

I am grateful for God's generosity and my commitment to be responsible with everything I have been given. I am grateful I can be helpful to others by my giving and not have an expectation for anything in return.

INTERCESSION:

I pray that others become faithful stewards of the resources God has entrusted to them, experiencing the joy and blessing of giving generously. I pray for God's provision in their lives and that any greed is replaced with a spirit of gratitude and generosity. May they clearly recognize moments of selfishness and instinctively respond with open hearts, reflecting God's love in all they do.

AMEN

Luke 12:5; Hebrews 13:5; John 15:13

DAY TWELVE
Resentment to Forgiveness

Bearing with one another, and forgiving each other, whoever has a complaint against anyone; just as the Lord forgave you, so must you do also.
Colossians 3:13, NASB

The term "resentment" comes from the French word *sentir*, meaning "to feel." It often refers to a recurring negative emotion and can arise from a multitude of circumstances, making it an almost inevitable part of human interaction. Factors such as a lack of support, trust, and intimacy, alongside conflict and neglect, can trigger these feelings. When we harbor resentment, we may find ourselves ensnared in anger or bitterness; if left unaddressed, these emotions can manifest as cold behaviors and emotional outbursts. The weight of resentment can create formidable barriers, distorting our perceptions and straining our relationships. Living in this emotional turmoil is arduous, but in our quest for healing, turning our focus toward God can illuminate the path forward.

In seeking God, we begin to understand that forgiveness is not only possible but essential for our spiritual and emotional well-being. It's crucial to recognize that forgiveness is more about our journey than it is about the actions of others. While there are instances where forgiveness can lead to reconciliation, there are also times when the healthiest option is to distance ourselves from those who have hurt us. Acknowledging our feelings requires courage, as it allows us to confront the hurt and understand its impact on our lives. When we take the time to reflect on our emotions, we create space for clarity and healing.

{ God has a divine plan for our lives, one that rises above the weight of resentment and invites us into peace and healing. }

By practicing forgiveness, we uncover a lasting sense of liberation. This freedom allows us to release the shackles of past grievances and opens our hearts to new possibilities. In embracing forgiveness, we not only heal ourselves but also create a pathway for grace to flow into our lives, guiding us toward deeper connections and a more fulfilling existence.

PETITION:

Lord, help me to believe I can forgive those who have wronged me. Help me embrace my past experiences, so I can move into resolution with a willingness to forgive. Help me understand that forgiveness is for my well-being. In embracing forgiveness, I turn over my pain to You, a God who sees me and cares for me.

GRATITUDE:

I am grateful for the willingness to forgive others. I am grateful that God provides direction on how to surrender my resentment and find forgiveness. I am grateful for a fresh perspective that grants a softened heart, which allows for a deeper understanding of resentment and how it isn't conducive to living a life of emotional freedom.

INTERCESSION:

I pray that anyone grappling with resentment will seek God for the strength to find resolution. May they find a new perspective through the lens of Your love and grace, enabling them to experience spiritual renewal. Help them lean into forgiveness and let go of past hurts, releasing the burden that resentment brings. As they surrender their pain to You, may they discover the freedom and healing that comes from a heart transformed by forgiveness. Let Your peace fill their hearts, guiding them toward reconciliation and restoration in their relationships.

AMEN

Ephesians 4:31-32; Mark 11:25; Matthew 6:14-15

DAY THIRTEEN
Distracted to Focused

But the worries of this life, the deceitfulness of wealth and the desires for other things come in and choke the word, making it unfruitful.
Mark 4:19, NIV

Distractions are an unavoidable reality of modern life, yet their effects can be deeply damaging. Often, distractions act as deliberate diversions, steering us away from our goals and responsibilities. How frequently do we catch ourselves scrolling through our phones instead of tackling the tasks we set out to accomplish? Distractions can also take the form of a wandering mind, causing us to lose focus on the matter at hand. Living in a state of distraction leaves us feeling aimless and may even lead us to stagnation. Over time, we may find ourselves settling for less, losing motivation, and neglecting our true potential.

In a world saturated with distractions, God invites us to seek clarity and maintain our focus. When we cultivate this focus, we can discern what truly matters and recognize the obstacles that hinder our progress. Our focus shapes our perspective, while clinging to distractions only diminishes our sense of purpose. To foster a genuine sense of direction, we must explore our deepest desires and identify what truly motivates us. By concentrating on our priorities, we can manage our time more effectively, gaining greater control over our energy and resources.

{ **As we develop the practice of prioritizing what is essential, we align ourselves with God's calling, opening ourselves to a future brimming with possibility.** }

By eliminating distractions, we not only clarify our path but also equip ourselves with the tools necessary to embrace the life God has designed for us. This journey toward intentional living paves the way for a more meaningful and purpose-driven life.

PETITION:

Lord, help me remove any mental clutter that may be holding me back from fully embracing Your calling on my life. Help me believe that You have predestined a unique purpose for me, and remind me of the importance of staying focused and not becoming distracted from my mission. I pray for consistency in my efforts and ask for Your strength to guide me each day. Grant me the diligence and determination needed to pursue my life's purpose wholeheartedly, trusting in Your plan and timing. Let my heart and mind be aligned with Your will, so I can walk confidently in the path You have set before me.

GRATITUDE:

I am grateful I can be mindful of any distractions that may lead me away from my God-given assignment. I am grateful for the mental capacity to focus on what's in front of me and release anything that can take me off course.

INTERCESSION:

I pray for others to develop the discipline needed to maintain focus in their lives. May they have the discernment to identify what truly matters and find a deep reliance on God to guide them toward full completion in their endeavors. I ask that God strengthen their resolve, helping them prioritize their goals and overcome distractions. In moments of uncertainty, may they remember to turn to God for clarity and direction, trusting He will equip them with everything they need to fulfill their purpose.

AMEN

Proverbs 4:25; Colossians 3:1-2; 1 Corinthians 7:35

DAY FOURTEEN
Manipulative to Authentic

Do not be deceived: God cannot be mocked. A man reaps what he sows.
Galatians 6:7, NIV

Manipulation involves the coercion or control of others to achieve personal objectives, often resulting in a web of mistrust, blurred boundaries, and ineffective communication. While most people may engage in manipulative behaviors at some point in their lives, it's crucial to recognize the subtlety of these actions. Passive aggression, gaslighting, selfish ambition, deceit, and withholding affection are all forms of manipulation that can inflict lasting damage on relationships. When manipulation becomes a habitual pattern, it undermines the foundation of healthy connections, isolating the manipulator and inflicting emotional turmoil on the manipulated.

If you find yourself caught in a cycle of manipulation, whether as the manipulator or the one being manipulated, acknowledging the issue is the first step toward healing. It may be wise to seek counsel and turn your circumstances over to God's care. Scripture provides a clear warning against deception, reminding us of the importance of walking in truth. Immersing ourselves in God's Word allows us to discern the difference between manipulation and genuine connection.

{ **Embracing authenticity is an act of self-preservation and love.** }

This may involve setting boundaries to safeguard our morals and personal space. At the same time, we must be vigilant against any behaviors that lack sincerity or fail to contribute positively to others. Living authentically means aligning our words, actions, and beliefs with our true selves, the person God created us to be. This integrity fosters trust and inspires loyalty in our relationships, revealing that God created us not just for connection but for meaningful and reciprocal interactions. Authenticity empowers us to embrace our uniqueness and live out God's purpose for us in relationships defined by sincerity and mutual respect.

PETITION:

Lord, help me search my heart for any ways I may have been manipulative in the past. Grant me the clarity to recognize how my actions may have affected others and guide me to align with Your statutes as I strive to walk in ways that are upright and just. If I have been manipulated or find myself in such a situation currently, grant me the courage to seek wise counsel and establish healthy boundaries. May I lean on Your wisdom and strength to navigate these challenges, trusting in Your guidance to lead me toward healing and truth.

GRATITUDE:

I am grateful for my ability to be authentic with myself and others. I am grateful that God honors those who walk with integrity. Although it may not always be easy, I know it is worthwhile. I am grateful I can foster authentic relationships because of my commitment to live with integrity.

INTERCESSION:

I pray others can heal from any harm caused by manipulation, finding the strength to move forward and reclaim their sense of self. May they develop the discernment to recognize what is true, enabling them to distinguish between genuine relationships and those that seek to exploit. I pray they find a community that is nurturing and authentic, a place where they can feel safe, loved, and supported in their healing journey. May this community uplift them and encourage them to grow in their faith, fostering connections that reflect Your love and grace.

AMEN

Proverbs 26:24-25; Ephesians 4:25; James 3:16

DAY FIFTEEN
Impatient to Patient

Rejoice in hope, be patient in tribulation, be constant in prayer.
Romans 12:12, ESV

The phrase "patience is a virtue" resonates with many, yet translating that into action can feel like an uphill battle. In our fast-paced world, we often yearn for immediacy, whether we're waiting for a text reply, seeking a promotion, or desiring clarity in our relationships. Unfortunately, impatience can have significant negative repercussions. Those who struggle with it may come across as insensitive, impulsive, or even arrogant. This destructive mindset can consume us, leading to behaviors that hinder our productivity at work and create friction in our personal interactions. Impatience breeds conflict, fuels rash reactions, and creates a cycle of irritation that gradually erodes our connections with others.

To effectively combat impatience, it's vital to recognize the triggers that provoke us and turn to God for guidance and strength. James 1:2-4 (NIV) reminds us, "Consider it pure joy, my brothers and sisters, whenever you face trials of many kinds, because you know that the testing of your faith produces perseverance. Let perseverance finish its work so that you may be mature and complete, not lacking anything." God calls us to practice patience with one another, reminding us that this quality often emerges through life's tests and trials. The ability to endure challenging situations and difficult individuals without losing our composure can lead to meaningful outcomes, helping us avoid self-centered actions we might later regret. By taking the time to assess the full context of a situation, we can create space for inner peace and nurture hope that everything will unfold according to God's plan. To be patient is to trust in His timing, which equips us to navigate life's challenges with grace and resilience.

While cultivating patience demands effort and intentionality, the rewards are immeasurable.

> **As we invest in this essential virtue, we foster deeper understanding and compassion within ourselves, enriching our lives and those around us.**

Romans 8:25 (NIV) reminds us, "But if we hope for what we do not yet have, we wait for it patiently." Patience empowers us to embrace life's uncertainties with a steady heart, enabling us to thrive in a world that often insists on immediate results.

PETITION:

Lord, help me to work on being patient, so I may be effective in both professional and personal relationships. Help me address the areas in my life where I am easily triggered to respond with impatience. Help me understand that patience is virtuous and better for my overall well-being. Grant me the wisdom to recognize the benefits of waiting and the strength to persevere during challenging times. May I learn to appreciate the journey, trusting in Your timing and plan for my life.

GRATITUDE:

I am grateful for God's perfect will for my life. I am grateful for God's counsel and my efforts to avoid making hasty decisions. I am grateful that I can be empathetic, kind, and cooperative.

INTERCESSION:

I pray for others to cultivate a spirit of patience in all areas of their lives, allowing them to navigate challenges with grace and understanding. Help them to become aware of their tendencies toward impatience, whether in relationships, work, or personal growth. May they find the strength to pause and reflect before reacting, embracing the journey rather than rushing toward the destination. Lord, teach them to trust in Your timing, knowing that each moment is an opportunity for growth and deeper faith. May they experience the peace that comes from surrendering to Your perfect plan.

AMEN

1 Corinthians 13:4-5; Galatians 5:22-23; Ephesians 4:1-3

DAY SIXTEEN
Withdrawn to Engaged

You make known to me the path of life; in your presence there is fullness of joy; at your right hand are pleasures forevermore.
Psalm 16:11, ESV

When we find ourselves withdrawn or shut down, it often stems from a desire to protect ourselves from potential hurt. Consider the example of a turtle: when it senses a threat, it instinctively retreats into its shell for safety. This physical response serves as a powerful metaphor for our emotional withdrawal. If we are caught in a cycle of conflict or are grappling with past traumas, our emotions can become frayed, making the prospect of communication feel overwhelming. As a defense mechanism, we may begin to bottle up our feelings and isolate ourselves, anticipating rejection or feeling unheard.

Our perceptions are deeply shaped by our past experiences. If we have endured turmoil or hardship, we might cope by distancing ourselves from others, believing this will shield us from further pain. However, this disconnect often leads to unhealthy coping mechanisms and creates barriers that hinder us from living within God's intended design for our relationships.

Conversely, when we embrace emotional engagement, we become attuned to our own feelings and those of the people around us. Living in this state means being intentional and present, allowing us to fully experience the moment. Developing effective communication skills is crucial for fostering a sense of meaning and value in our lives. God created us for connection, and our spirits flourish when we invest in relationships that embody mutual effort and care.

Building and maintaining these connections requires courage and determination.

> **Emotional engagement is essential; it enables us to cultivate trust and forge deeper bonds with others.**

Through our commitment to being present and intentional, we unlock a fullness of life that can only be realized through meaningful relationships.

PETITION:

Lord, help me to fully experience Your goodness in my life and remind me that I am called by name, treasured, and loved by You. While I understand the importance of establishing healthy boundaries for my well-being, grant me the discernment to identify what truly needs my attention. Help me recognize areas where I may be withdrawn or distant, allowing me to reconnect with others and draw closer to You. May Your Spirit guide me in creating a balance between safeguarding my heart and actively engaging in relationships that reflect Your love and grace.

GRATITUDE:

I am grateful for a willing heart to engage in a balanced life. I am grateful that God created me out of love and for the purpose of sharing love. Today, I am grateful I don't have to hide from conflict and can engage the people that God has placed in my life.

INTERCESSION:

I pray others will begin to recognize if they have prematurely withdrawn from people, places, or things. I pray they can find the wisdom to healthfully engage and rely on God to order their steps. I pray for restoration where it is needed and a full reliance on God for endurance and bravery.

AMEN

2 Corinthians 12:9; Psalm 46:1-3; Isaiah 41:10

DAY SEVENTEEN
Dishonest to Honest

Truthful lips endure forever, but a lying tongue is but for a moment.
Proverbs 12:19, ESV

People have an incredible ability to justify their actions, often leading to self-deception and dishonesty towards others. Whether driven by a desire for self-preservation or the fear of causing pain, this dishonesty creates a deceptive sense of control that ultimately results in negative consequences. Various factors can lead someone to engage in deceit. Fear of repercussions, shame over past mistakes, or the urge to maintain a façade are all potential offenders. Yet the truth remains: deceit is always revealed in time. When we lie to others, we jeopardize our relationships; when we lie to ourselves, we compromise our moral integrity. Dishonesty can become a learned behavior, and without corrective measures, it may result in emotional turmoil as our words and actions clash. In our pursuit of authenticity, we must turn to God's teachings, seeking to live blamelessly and walk with integrity.

Honesty is foundational for nurturing meaningful relationships with both God and others. It aligns us with the divine intention for our lives and serves as a direct reflection of our character. Proverbs 12:22 (NIV) reminds us, "The Lord detests lying lips, but he delights in people who are trustworthy."

> **Our character shapes the trajectory of our lives and is essential for discovering our true purpose.**

Created in the image of God, we are called to uphold a

clear conscience. While honesty can be challenging and requires continual effort, it extends beyond our interactions with others; it also encompasses our internal narrative. If we repeatedly tell ourselves that we are unworthy or inadequate, we perpetuate self-deception.

By honestly evaluating our worth and capabilities, we can approach life with renewed confidence and engage with others in integrity. As Ephesians 4:25 (NIV) encourages us, "Therefore each of you must put off falsehood and speak truthfully to your neighbor, for we are all members of one body." Embracing honesty not only deepens our relationships but also allows us to step into our true identities as beloved children of God, fostering deeper connections and authentic relationships.

PETITION:

Lord, help me to fully embrace life in all its complexities, so I can experience the true freedom that comes from living authentically. Give me the courage to practice honesty, especially in situations where it feels difficult or uncomfortable. May I rely on Your guidance to navigate these challenges, trusting that Your truth will illuminate my path. Help me to cultivate a spirit of transparency, knowing that living in accordance with Your principles not only liberates me but also encourages those around me to seek a similar honesty. Lead me to be a vessel of Your truth, reflecting Your love in every interaction and decision.

GRATITUDE:

I am grateful for being made in the image of God and for the drive to live honestly. I am grateful I can look to God for refinement and believe that God's desires for my life are good.

INTERCESSION:

I pray God will guide others to cultivate a spirit of honesty within their hearts. May they become attuned to any dishonest thoughts that may arise, recognizing the importance of surrendering these thoughts and embracing the truth. I pray for the courage to confront and rectify any situations affected by falsehood, allowing honesty to mend relationships and restore integrity. May they find strength in vulnerability and boldness in their pursuit of truth, trusting that God's guidance will lead them to genuine connections and a more fulfilling life.

AMEN

Proverbs 12:22; Psalm 101:7; Colossians 3:9

DAY EIGHTEEN
Impulsivity to Self-Control

To make rash, hasty decisions shows that you are not trusting the Lord. But when you rely totally on God, you will still act carefully and prudently.
Proverbs 28:25, TPT

Impulsivity is the tendency to act on a whim, often without pausing to consider the consequences. This behavior can manifest in a wide spectrum, from harmless spontaneity to reckless decisions that overlook the needs and safety of ourselves and others. While a degree of impulsivity might infuse our lives with adventure and openness, unchecked impulsive behaviors can create turmoil, hindering healthy decision-making and negatively impacting our relationships and overall well-being.

When we act impulsively, we risk conflict and distress, both for ourselves and those around us. The repeated cycle of impulsive decisions can leave us feeling trapped, leading to regret and frustration. To break free from this cycle, it's essential to address the underlying issues driving our impulsivity and trust in God's guidance as we seek to fulfill His perfect will for our lives.

Living in a relationship with God is a desire many of us have, yet it can feel overwhelming, especially when faced with hardships. Surrendering our ways and learning to follow His direction requires us to embrace self-control, which involves exercising restraint and moderation in all areas of our lives. For instance, taking a moment to pause before reacting can prevent us from saying something we might later regret, preserving our relationships and our peace of mind.

God desires to empower us to lead lives marked by moderation and self-control in our actions, speech, and thoughts.

> **A crucial aspect of cultivating self-control lies within our minds, and our thoughts often dictate our actions.**

By meditating on God's Word, we nurture our spiritual health and reinforce our capacity for self-restraint. As we choose to make wise decisions grounded in faith, we can experience transformative results, paving the way for a fulfilling life aligned with God's purpose. In this journey, we learn self-control is not just about restraint; it's about living intentionally and harmoniously, reflecting God's love and grace in every aspect of our lives.

PETITION:

Lord, I ask for Your guidance in making decisions with caution and thoughtfulness. Help me to pause and reflect before I act, ensuring my choices align with Your will. In moments of difficulty, grant me the grace to practice tolerance and understanding. Lead me deeper into Your peace and presence, so I may be a true extension of Your love and light in the world. May my actions reflect Your character and bring glory to Your name.

GRATITUDE:

I am grateful for the ability to exercise restraint and rely on God for self-control. I am grateful that God goes before me in all I do and that I am not responsible for forcing decisions or outcomes. I am grateful that God is all-knowing and there is nothing I can do to separate me from God's love.

INTERCESSION:

I pray others will discover the strength to operate from a place of self-control, even in challenging circumstances. May they feel equipped through Your divine guidance and wisdom to respond with careful consideration when faced with tests and trials. Help them recognize the importance of pausing before reacting, allowing Your Spirit to lead them in their decisions. I pray they will cultivate patience and discernment, trusting that their reliance on You will empower them to act in ways that reflect Your love and grace.

AMEN

Ecclesiastes 5:2; Proverbs 14:29; Acts 19:36

DAY NINETEEN
Defeated to Victorious

We are hard pressed on every side, but not crushed; perplexed, but not in despair; persecuted, but not abandoned; struck down, but not destroyed.
2 Corinthians 4:8-9, NIV

Our daily struggles often run deep, rooted in a spiritual battle we may not always recognize. The reality is an enemy seeking to keep us defeated, unarmed with the powerful truth of God. When we surrender our potential, we may find ourselves seeking satisfaction in lesser things, merely going through the motions without any real passion or purpose. Additionally, our past mistakes can plant seeds of shame, convincing us we are unworthy of God's grace and love. When we allow this mindset to take hold, we are choosing to live in defeat, potentially leaving our fellowship with God in the rearview mirror and making ourselves easy targets for spiritual attacks.

Yet, in God's unwavering love and faithfulness, He has equipped us with everything we need to engage in this battle. Every day, we must consciously put on the full armor of God, as described in Ephesians 6:13-17, preparing ourselves to push back against the enemy's agenda. Establishing a daily rhythm of prayer and immersing ourselves in God's Word is crucial to our strategy for victory. Even in those moments when we feel far from God, our identity remains unaltered. We are all predestined for greatness, and it brings comfort to know that before we even saw the light of day, God had holy plans for each of us (Jeremiah 1:5).

{ **In embracing our weaknesses, we find that God's perfect strength can shine through us.** }

space for God to guide us on our journey. This act of surrender is a courageous expression of faith, allowing us to trust in God's sovereignty even when life feels particularly challenging. By relinquishing what we cannot change and focusing on what lies ahead, we can cultivate a hopeful perspective, believing God is weaving all things together for our good, as promised in Romans 8:28 (NIV).

Letting go does not equate to dismissing our past. Instead, it encourages us to make less room for negative thoughts and emotions, freeing us from the weight of burdens we were never meant to carry. As we find this newfound balance, we develop resilience and submit our lives wholeheartedly to God. By entrusting our desires and plans to Him, we align ourselves with His will—a plan that goes beyond our limited understanding and brings us peace in the midst of uncertainty. In doing so, we not only release our burdens, but also open ourselves to the abundant life God intends for us, as Jesus assures in John 10:10 (ESV): "The thief comes only to steal and kill and destroy. I came that they may have life and have it abundantly.

PETITION:

Lord, I ask You to help me release the desire to control my life and circumstances. Guide me in stepping aside so I may fully embrace Your will. Instruct me on how to live in Your truth and by Your Spirit. Help me to surrender my worries and anxieties, allowing me to trust in Your perfect plan. Open my heart to the new things You are doing in my life, and grant me the wisdom to recognize and embrace these changes. May I find peace in the journey of faith, knowing You are guiding me every step of the way.

GRATITUDE:

I am grateful God is the keeper of my path. I am grateful I can surrender freely and rely on God for a sense of peace that can grow within me day by day.

INTERCESSION:

I pray others can experience an increase in steadfast faith, trusting wholeheartedly that God is in control of every aspect of their lives. May they seek Him earnestly in their times of need, finding comfort and strength in His presence. Help them to embrace the understanding that God's timing is always perfect, even when it seems difficult to comprehend. As they navigate through challenges, I ask that their faith be fortified, allowing them to rest in the assurance that He is working all things together for their good. May they find peace in surrendering their worries to Him, knowing that His plans are greater than their own.

AMEN

Psalm 46:10; Ephesians 3:20; Isaiah 26:3

DAY TWENTY-ONE
Rebellious to Obedient

If you are willing and obedient, you will eat the good things of the land.
Isaiah 1:19, NIV

Rebellion is not just a simple act of defiance; it is a disconnection from the divine order established by God. Driven by a false sense of superiority, rebellion emerges from a heart which has strayed into pride, as Scripture warns us: "Live in harmony with one another. Do not be haughty, but associate with the lowly. Never be wise in your own sight" (Romans 12:16, ESV). When we prioritize our desires over divine authority, we sever ourselves from the source of true wisdom and disrupt the rhythms of life meant to guide us toward fulfillment.

Understanding the roots of our rebellion requires honest introspection. It may arise from personal struggles, societal pressures, or unresolved conflicts, but at its core lies a longing for control and autonomy that blinds us to God's intended design. When we resist this design—whether through our actions or our hearts—we invite spiritual decline and forfeit the richness of God's promises. Yet, there is always hope: reconciliation with our Creator is not just a possibility; it is an invitation to transform our lives from the inside out.

> **Opening our hearts to God means embracing the truth of His goodness and sovereignty.**

He desires a relationship built on trust, love, and obedience, where submission is not a sign of weakness, but a pathway to true strength. This journey often requires us to step beyond our comfort zones, confronting fears and relinquishing our illusions of control. While our human limitations may cause us to doubt our ability to follow His lead, we must remember that with God's supernatural strength, all things are possible.

Obedience becomes an act of surrender that reflects our faith in God's perfect plan. It invites us into a deeper understanding of our purpose and identity as beloved children of the Creator. As we yield to His will, we find ourselves aligning with a divine narrative that transcends our immediate circumstances, guiding us toward a life of integrity and meaning. In embracing God's wisdom, we unlock the potential to live without compromise, fully engaged in the richness of our relationship with Him, and empowered to navigate the complexities of life with grace and purpose.

PETITION:

Lord, heal my heart and renew my strength. Help me identify if there is any stubbornness or disobedience in my heart so I can change my ways. Help me to rid any rebellious thoughts and become more aware of your guidance.

GRATITUDE:

I am grateful for the ability to yield to God's will, trusting His perfect plan over my own desires. Surrendering to Him brings peace and freedom, knowing His ways are higher and His purposes are always for my good. I am thankful for the grace that allows me to let go of control and align my heart with His, experiencing the fullness of His guidance and provision in every aspect of my life.

INTERCESSION:

I pray others can trust deeply in the goodness of God's love, knowing it is unwavering and unconditional. May they have the wisdom to recognize the voice of rebellion that seeks to lead them astray. Help them to discern the truth and rely on God for a renewed mind, one that reflects His grace and purpose. I ask that they experience the transformative power of His love in their hearts, enabling them to live boldly and confidently in His promises.

AMEN

1 Samuel 15:23, Jeremiah 5:23, Hebrews 10:26

DAY TWENTY-TWO
Shameful to Virtuous

Instead of your shame you will receive a double portion, and instead of disgrace you will rejoice in your inheritance. And so you will inherit a double portion in your land, and everlasting joy will be yours.
Isaiah 61:7, NIV

Shame often leaves us feeling defeated and diminished, creating a chasm between our authentic selves and the world around us. This insidious emotion not only isolates us but also undermines our self-image, leading us to perceive ourselves as flawed and unworthy. Rooted in experiences of rejection, neglect, or embarrassment, shame lays bare our vulnerabilities, pushing us toward destructive behaviors. Throughout history, it has ensnared humanity in a painful cycle of failure and pride. Yet, it's crucial to understand that shame does not define us; with God's guidance, we can transcend it.

The journey to breaking the grip of shame begins with acknowledging God's greatness and trusting Him as our ultimate source of virtue and truth. As we lean on God as our provider, we weaken shame's hold on our lives. This reliance empowers us to uphold our values and moral standards, reminding us of our inherent worth. As Psalm 139:14 (NIV) reminds us, "I praise you because I am fearfully and wonderfully made; your works are wonderful, I know that full well." By embracing virtues such as honesty, integrity, kindness, compassion, and service, we align our actions with the principles of righteousness. Cultivating these positive habits allows us to stand firm in our convictions, even in the face of rejection. In doing so, we find that leading a virtuous life not only enriches our own existence but also nurtures harmony in our relationships with others.

> As we progress on this journey toward healing, we must remember that each step taken in faith draws us closer to a life liberated from the chains of shame.

We are invited to embrace our true identities as beloved creations of God, capable of reflecting His love and grace in a world that often feels unforgiving. Ephesians 2:10 (NIV) reminds us, "For we are God's handiwork, created in Christ Jesus to do good works, which God prepared in advance for us to do." In this divine embrace, we find the courage to live authentically, allowing our lives to shine brightly with the hope and redemption that only God can provide.

In 1 John 1:9 (NIV), we are reassured, "If we confess our sins, He is faithful and just and will forgive us our sins and purify us from all unrighteousness." This promise not only reassures us that shame can be replaced with grace but also invites us into a renewed sense of purpose and belonging. Moreover, Romans 8:1 (ESV) proclaims, "There is therefore now no condemnation for those who are in Christ Jesus." This powerful truth invites us to let go of shame and step into the light of God's love, which empowers us to embrace our true identities as cherished children of God.

PETITION:

Lord, help me to see Your movement in every detail of my life and to trust in Your promise to keep me in perfect peace. Remind me daily that my identity is found in You alone, and I am defined by Your love and grace, not by my past or my failures. Help me to let go of any shame or guilt that may be blocking me from fully experiencing Your Spirit, so I may walk in freedom and be morally well, reflecting Your goodness in all I do.

GRATITUDE:

I am grateful that God's Word is faithful and true. I am grateful I am more precious than rubies (Proverbs 3:15, NIV). I am grateful for the desire to serve God well and to behold God's grace.

INTERCESSION:

I pray that others may be molded into the individuals God has created them to be. Help them grasp what is holy and good. May they come to understand that acting in accordance with what is right is essential for a flourishing and fulfilling life.

AMEN

Revelation 16:15; 2 Corinthians 4:2; Jude 1:13

DAY TWENTY-THREE
Destructive to Constructive

And let us consider how to stir up one another to love and good works, not neglecting to meet together, as is the habit of some, but encouraging one another, and all the more as you see the Day drawing near.
Hebrews 10:24-25, ESV

Destructive behaviors can manifest in various forms, impacting both our physical and mental health. Often, these actions are symptoms of deeper emotional struggles influenced by factors such as environment, anxiety, depression, temptation, and low self-esteem. Importantly, there is no one-size-fits-all explanation for these behaviors; each person's journey is unique, and uncovering the root causes may require time and introspection. Subtly destructive behaviors can emerge from a buildup of distorted beliefs that do not align with God's truth. When our hearts are torn between worldly influences and a relationship with God, we can find ourselves entangled in self-destructive patterns. Without self-awareness and divine guidance, we risk becoming trapped by these harmful behaviors. Thus, in our pursuit of a fulfilling and purposeful life, it is crucial to seek Godly wisdom and provision.

To actively prevent a life marked by destruction, we can commit ourselves to spiritual growth while adhering to fundamental biblical principles. A key goal in living a Godly life is to uplift ourselves and those around us with the truth. This begins with being intentional about our actions and words. We must ask ourselves: Are we speaking life into our own thoughts and those of others, or are we sowing seeds of discord? Are we living in a way that encourages and empowers those around us, or are we inadvertently causing chaos and discouragement? Proverbs 18:21 (NIV) states, "The tongue has the power of life and death, and those who love it will eat its fruit."

> **By reflecting on our intentions and allowing the Holy Spirit to guide us, we can cultivate goodness in our hearts, becoming vessels of God's love and embodying our new identities in Christ.**

Raised to new life through grace, we can confidently live in alignment with God's plan and purpose for us. As we embrace the truth of our identity in Christ, we see that 2 Corinthians 5:17 (NIV) declares, "Therefore, if anyone is in Christ, the new creation has come: The old has gone, the new is here!" This transformative truth empowers us to break free from the chains of destructive behavior and embrace a life characterized by hope, healing, and purpose. Through prayer, scripture, and community, we can continually seek to align our lives with God's will, fostering an environment of love and support that encourages growth and resilience.

PETITION:

Lord, help me renew my trust in You alone. Show me the areas in my life where I can take responsibility, and help me place my life fully in Your hands. Remind me, You are always faithful to rescue and protect me from the ways of the world. Guide my steps so I am in the right places at the right time, allowing me to be a light to others.

GRATITUDE:

I am grateful for God's forgiveness and hope because of my openness to receive direction and provision. I am grateful for God's omniscience and that God's compassion meets our needs if we are on the brink of destruction. I am grateful I can take refuge in God and establish my steps with God's Word.

INTERCESSION:

I pray for others to be protected under the shadow of God's wing. I pray for those who have been impacted by the destructive ways of others and for God to bring justice where it is needed. I pray for protection against harmful influences and for help to live a new life in God's purpose. I pray for others to abide in the instructions laid out in God's Word and to experience a renewal of spirit.

AMEN

1 Thessalonians 5:11; Ephesians 4:29; Psalm 55:23

DAY TWENTY-FOUR
Stubborn to Flexible

For the time is coming when people will not endure sound teaching, but having itching ears they will accumulate for themselves teachers to suit their own passions.
2 Timothy 4:3, ESV

At the core of stubbornness often lies a fear of letting go (our ideas, beliefs, or even aspects of our identity). While stubbornness itself isn't inherently negative, it can become problematic when it obscures our ability to recognize our shortcomings and reevaluate our emotions. Sometimes, this rigidity emerges from a clear vision of what we want; other times, it springs from an overwhelming need to have things our way. This creates a fine line between being driven and motivated and being difficult or obstinate.

We can cling too tightly to our views, insisting on our course of action, even in the face of evidence that we may be wrong. It's essential to examine the underlying motivations for this stubbornness. Such resistance can stifle our growth and maturity, making it difficult to adapt to new circumstances. Proverbs 12:15 (NIV) reminds us, "The way of fools seems right to them, but the wise listen to advice."

To cultivate a healthier perspective, we must embrace resilience and flexibility. This adaptability is crucial, particularly on our spiritual journeys. Our understanding of control and our moral actions, especially concerning the well-being of others, play a significant role in our spiritual development. As Romans 12:2 (NIV) encourages us, "Do not conform to the pattern of this world, but be transformed by the renewing of your mind . . ."

Mental and emotional flexibility are fundamental in nurturing our faith and relationships.

> **Recognizing God is in control allows us to accept what we cannot change, fostering greater adaptability in our thoughts and actions.**

Philippians 4:6-7 (NIV) states, "Do not be anxious about anything, but in every situation, by prayer and petition, with thanksgiving, present your requests to God. And the peace of God, which transcends all understanding, will guard your hearts and your minds in Christ Jesus."

By approaching life's challenges with trust in God and an open heart, we cultivate the belief that most situations can be resolved and improved. Investing in adjusting our responses to align with our circumstances can strengthen our faith and lead to a newfound sense of freedom. This journey not only enriches our spiritual lives but also deepens our connections with others, paving the way for growth, understanding, and lasting fulfillment, as emphasized in Ephesians 4:2-3 (NIV): "Be completely humble and gentle; be patient, bearing with one another in love. Make every effort to keep the unity of the Spirit through the bond of peace."

PETITION:

Lord, help me stay close to You in times of uncertainty. When I don't know which way to turn or how to respond, guide me into rightful action. Help me become aware of where I need to be more flexible and give me the courage to trust in Your will and timing. Help me lead with humility, so I can experience God's fullness and mercy in everything I do.

GRATITUDE:

I am grateful for God's continual grace and that God is available to those who humble themselves. I am grateful for the opportunity to change my approach in areas I may have been too stringent in before.

INTERCESSION:

God, I lift up those who are facing conflict due to stubbornness. I pray they may gain the awareness of their need for You in their lives. Help them recognize how their unwillingness to let go or compromise may be hindering their relationships and spiritual growth. Grant them the humility to submit to Your purpose for their lives and to seek reconciliation with others. May they find the strength to overcome their pride and be open to Your guidance, allowing Your love and wisdom to permeate their hearts. Help them to embrace the peace which comes from aligning their will with Yours and to foster relationships rooted in understanding and compassion.

AMEN

Matthew 12:30; Matthew 17:16-20; Romans 2:5

DAY TWENTY-FIVE
Irresponsible to Responsible

So whoever knows the right thing to do and fails to do it, for him it is a sin.
James 4:17, ESV

Irresponsible behavior lacks congruence with who God calls us to be, and if we aren't careful, our spiritual health will go untended. Whether our irresponsibility is occasional or habitual, unwanted consequences are likely. In our pleasure-seeking culture, it's easy to become self-absorbed and sidetracked into living irresponsibly, taking us further from our purpose. If we are irresponsible in our relationships, we will be seen as untrustworthy and unreliable. Without dependability, we will never develop the self-discipline and care needed to have meaningful relationships. If we are irresponsible in our workplace or with our resources, then our livelihood can suffer greatly, leaving us ill-equipped to take care of ourselves. Whatever role we find ourselves in, trusting God enough to practice obedience to His principles will avoid the consequences of carelessness and afford us blessings that reflect a responsible lifestyle.

We have a duty to uphold the affairs we've been given in this life. Accepting responsibility for our lives is foundational in our orientation. We ALL have a responsibility to God. If we are parents, then we should be contributing to our families. If we are employees, then we should be diligent at work. Scripture tells us not to be deceived and that God cannot be mocked, for a man reaps what he sows (Galatians 6:7, ESV). There may be barriers keeping us from executing our responsibilities fully, but the willingness to step up and commit is what matters.

> **God's desire is for us to be good stewards of everything we have.**

God calls us to live responsibly in the way we act towards others (Luke 10:30-37, ESV), the way we treat our families (1 Timothy 5:8, ESV), studying God's Word (2 Timothy 2:15, ESV), and the way we handle money (Hebrews 13:5, NIV).

PETITION:

Lord, I come before You with a humble heart, seeking Your guidance and strength. Help me to embrace the duties You have entrusted to me with joy and faithfulness. Grant me the wisdom to discern my responsibilities and the courage to carry them out in a way that pleases You. Let every action I take be done in harmony with Your perfect will, reflecting Your love and purpose. May my life glorify You in all things.

GRATITUDE:

I am grateful I can be responsible for the way I show up in life. I am grateful God gives me examples in His written Word for how to behave. I am grateful that my thoughts, actions, and words reflect my commitment to living in God's Will.

INTERCESSION:

Lord, I pray that others may embrace responsibility as a core value in their lives. May they recognize the importance of being accountable for their actions, decisions, and the resources You have entrusted to them. Help them take responsibility where it is needed, whether in their relationships, work, or personal growth. May they understand that being faithful with what You have given them not only honors You, but also contributes to their growth and the well-being of those around them. Guide them to act with integrity and purpose, fostering a spirit of stewardship that reflects Your love and grace.

AMEN

Proverbs 13:17; Matthew 6:33; Proverbs 6:16-19

DAY TWENTY-SIX
Hopeless to Hopeful

For I am convinced that neither death nor life, neither angels nor demons, neither the present nor the future, nor any powers, neither height nor depth, nor anything else in all creation, will be able to separate us from the love of God that is in Christ Jesus our Lord.
Romans 8:38-39, NIV

Hopelessness is a powerful emotion that can leave us feeling dismal and disconnected, often causing us to lose interest in what once brought us joy. Without hope, every challenge can seem overwhelming. When personal struggles collide with the relentless demands of the world, they can create a whirlwind of despair, leaving devastation in their wake. This feeling is often accompanied by a lack of inspiration, powerlessness, isolation, and oppression, and it typically signals deeper issues that require our attention.

To alleviate this emotional turmoil, we can seek insight and support from both others and God. As Psalm 46:1 (NIV) assures us, "God is our refuge and strength, an ever-present help in trouble." We can lean on Him during difficult times. Even when the clouds of hopelessness obscure the good in our lives, it's vital to recognize that, like faith, hope can be cultivated through the Word of God. Romans 10:17 (KJV) teaches us, "So then faith cometh by hearing, and hearing by the Word of God."

In Psalm 78, God commands His people to recount the stories of His power and intervention, specifically so that future generations would "set their hope in God." If we allow ourselves to be held captive by hopelessness in isolation, we risk missing opportunities to nurture our hope through fellowship and to witness how God has restored others from despair.

It's essential to understand that anchoring our hope in worldly things (money, status, jobs, or relationships) can inevitably lead to disappointment. Instead, God calls us to set our minds on things that are above, not on things that are on earth (Colossians 3:2).

> **Hope is not merely a fleeting feeling; it is a deliberate choice to hold fast to the truths of Scripture.**

Hope in God is an inherent trust that empowers us to take steps leading to genuine joy and freedom. It redefines what is probable and illuminates pathways to the seemingly impossible. With our hope anchored in God, all things become possible, as Matthew 19:26 (NIV) reminds us: " . . . With man this is impossible, but with God all things are possible."

In this way, hope becomes not just a feeling but a transformative force, guiding us through life's challenges and drawing us closer to the peace and fulfillment that only God can provide.

PETITION:

Lord, help me take You at Your Word. Fill me with joy and peace as I trust in You. "For God alone, O my soul, waits in silence, for my hope is from him. He only is my rock and my salvation, my fortress; I shall not be shaken." (Psalm 62:5-6, ESV).

GRATITUDE:

I am grateful for an inspiring community. I am grateful others have gone before me and can be examples of how to overcome hopelessness. I am grateful I am never too far gone for God. God's promises are for me, and I can trust that I have a bright future ahead.

INTERCESSION:

I pray for others to put their hope and trust in God. I pray they understand that God will never leave them or forsake them (Hebrews 13:5, ESV) and that He always provides. I pray others will give God whatever is going on in their hearts. I pray for their strength and that God will fill them with hope as He guides their steps.

AMEN

2 Corinthians 1:3-4; John 14:27; Matthew 6:26

DAY TWENTY-SEVEN
Vindictive to Compassionate

Do not take revenge, my dear friends, but leave room for God's wrath, for it is written: "It is mine to avenge; I will repay," says the Lord.
Romans 12:19, NIV

Carrying the weight of vengeance hampers interpersonal relationships and is contradictory to the Bible's teaching of love, peace, and forgiveness. To be vengeful is to deny ourselves the opportunity to experience the fullness of love within ourselves and others. It can be extremely negative to harbor feelings of reprisal and revenge. Vindictiveness should not be accommodated by our moral compasses and instead should be replaced with the desire to extend grace and love. Dealing with conflicts and situations in the world is inevitable, but how we respond can make all the difference. Exercising self-control and practicing restraint is a battle we are all familiar with, but it is crucial in our pursuit of God's Will, "like a city that is broken into and without walls, is a man who has no control over his spirit" (Proverbs 25:28, NASB). If we let vindictiveness build in our hearts, we will eventually direct it towards others from a place of anger. An act of vindictiveness may seem justified, but the truth is, vengeance is not for us. Vindictiveness is in direct opposition to both the desires of God and the new mind we are trying to develop, and our primary task is to leave it in God's hands and seek to extend compassion and forgiveness.

When we take a deeper look at what compassion means, it encourages us to have mercy for others, even if we feel wronged. Compassion helps us stay connected with others, mending relationships where needed.

> **When we can move forward in compassion, we foster emotional intelligence and create an opportunity to make a difference in someone else's life.**

Others can reap the rewards of feeling understood and cared for. Developing compassion is a skillset associated with a wide range of positive behaviors, including prosocial behavior and conflict resolution. As a result, people who can extend compassion will be more content in their lives. This benefits both personal and professional relationships and contributes to the health of our spiritual well-being. Most importantly, "The Lord is gracious and compassionate, slow to anger and rich in love" (Psalm 145:8, NIV). God will always meet our needs, and we can take great comfort knowing compassion is at the heart of who God is.

PETITION:

Lord, help me grow in Your grace and kindness. Help me to be patient with those around me and to show compassion to those in need. Help me identify areas that need mending and give me the strength and wisdom to see everyone through Your eyes.

GRATITUDE:

I am grateful for God's love and care, for He is my constant companion and comforter. I am grateful for God's goodness and the ability to be an extension of God's compassion. I am grateful I can find peace and security in God's constant support and, in turn, be what others need.

INTERCESSION:

I pray others can seek guidance from God and tend to those who need to be given grace and compassion. I pray God will enlighten their hearts and give them the courage to face any difficulties currently separating them from God's love.

AMEN

2 Corinthians 12:10; Malachi 4:1; Acts 17: 24-28

DAY TWENTY-EIGHT
Self-Centered to Considerate

Do nothing from selfish ambition or conceit, but in humility count others more significant than yourselves. Let each of you look not only to his own interests, but also to the interests of others.
Philippians 2:3-4, ESV

Living self-centeredly is a barrier to forming healthy connections with others. If we can't show empathy and understanding for others' needs and feelings, then our relationships can become one-sided and dysfunctional. We may be more likely to take, rather than give; through time, our communal connections will become devoid of care and consideration.

Self-centeredness is costly. Living without room for God and other relationships naturally thwarts our ability to love others. Without providing proper support and consideration, we become less effective, and the quality of our relationships can suffer. Accompanied with poor support is a lack of self-awareness and lower levels of compassion. Consequently, we may be perceived as insensitive or unkind. While this may not be our intention, there is so much growth and transformation that can take place when we become self-aware and seek to understand God's relational design.

God calls us to be kind to one another (Hebrews 10:24, ESV). He wants us to put considerate love into practice and fill our hearts with goodness and self-control (Galatians 5:22, ESV). We are to "count others more significant than [our]selves" and to be humble, lowering ourselves so God can be glorified (Philippians 2:3, ESV). When we think of others, it can be in small, practical ways, like being of service or simply saying "hello."

> **Thinking of the benefit we can provide others is vitally important in being an extension of God's love.**

Our love for others is reflected in our consideration of them and is a deep aspect of heavenly wisdom. May we be a people of love, leaving a great impact on the lives of everyone around us.

PETITION:

Lord, help me hear Your invitation to deeply care for others. Help me love with greater love and reflect the image of You as I love others. Help me recognize Your boundless wisdom and love. Help me balance care and consideration for others with my needs and desires. Open my eyes to see beyond my own experiences and inspire my actions.

GRATITUDE:

I am grateful that God has created us finite in His good design. I am humbled by God's love and that nothing can separate me from His love. I am grateful God's Spirit lives within me, and that God has reshaped my heart to live out the love He's shown me through Christ.

INTERCESSION:

I pray others find wholeness in Your love, Lord, that they know they are fully seen, known and cherished by You. Let Your love heal their hearts, bring peace to their minds, and fill every empty place. As they rest in You, may they love others with the same grace and kindness You have shown them. Teach them to freely forgive fully and walk in the fullness of Your peace.

AMEN

1 Corinthians 13:4-5; James 3:14-16; 1 John 3:17

DAY TWENTY-NINE
Idolatry to Truth

Dear children, keep away from anything that might take God's place in your hearts.
1 John 5:21, NLT

When we think of idols, our minds often drift to graven images or figurines, yet idols extend far beyond mere representations of false gods. An idol is anything we treasure more than God, manifesting in relationships, attachments to political ideologies, material possessions, social media, and even in our self-image. These idols shape our thoughts and actions, and if we aren't vigilant, they can usurp God's rightful place as the center of our worship, disrupting the singular devotion for which we were created.

Often, our affections are directed toward good things, but the error arises when we assign greater importance to the created rather than the Creator. As stated in Romans 1:25 (NIV), "They exchanged the truth about God for a lie, and worshiped and served created things rather than the Creator. . ." When these created things become our ultimate focus, we inadvertently diminish God's sovereignty in our lives. Our attention shifts from seeking fulfillment in God to chasing the fleeting and inadequate pleasures of the world. We may convince ourselves that if we only had more money, more friends, or a different job, we would finally achieve contentment. This misplaced priority can manifest in various ways, highlighting the necessity of intentional reflection to discern what we may be idolizing. To fight against idolatry, we must first recognize and name our idols, for we cannot dismantle what we do not acknowledge.

Overcoming idolatry requires repositioning God to His rightful place in our hearts. As stated in Exodus 20:3 (ESV), "You shall have no other gods before me." He cannot be secondary to anything or anyone else, which is why He commands us not to make idols. God knows that any idol we create will ultimately lead to disappointment; true satisfaction cannot be found in the things of this world, no matter how appealing they may seem. When we genuinely believe that God is the ultimate source of goodness, we naturally desire His ways above all else. As Psalm 37:4 (ESV) declares, "Delight yourself in the Lord, and he will give you the desires of your heart."

> **We face a choice: we can either surrender to the pursuit of worldly things or redirect our energy toward the One who created everything.**

Our freedom and joy are found only in the fullness of devotion and worship toward Him, the source of all fulfillment. As Psalm 16:11 (ESV) reminds us, "You make known to me the path of life; in your presence there is fullness of joy; at your right hand are pleasures forevermore."

PETITION:

Lord, help me to break any connections I have with idols and reveal to me where I have misplaced my heart's affection. Show me any areas where I have elevated good things above You, and keep me from worshiping the blessings in my life instead of the One who gives them. Teach me to reject anything that pulls me away from Your presence and to surrender fully to Your will. I ask for conviction through Your grace, that I may clearly see the truth and keep my eyes focused solely on what is pure, noble, and eternal. Draw my heart closer to You each day, that my life may reflect Your glory.

GRATITUDE:

I am grateful for joyful repentance and that God binds my wandering heart to His truth. I am grateful that God knows me on my best days and my worst days and that nothing separates me from God's love. I am grateful that God's Spirit can help me discover idols in my life and that, in strength, I can turn away from them.

INTERCESSION:

God, help others in removing any idols from their hearts and replace them with greater love for You. Bring Your conviction when they are off course and Godly wisdom on how to move forward. Keep them from chasing things of the world and help them draw closer to Your heart.

AMEN

Colossians 3:5; Jonah 2:8; Galatians 4:8

DAY THIRTY
Doubt to Faith

Now faith is the assurance of things hoped for, the conviction of things not seen.
Hebrews 11:1, ESV

The book of James poignantly illustrates the nature of doubt, describing it as "a wave of the sea that is driven and tossed by the wind" (James 1:6, ESV). At its core, doubt represents a lack of steadfast confidence, casting shadows over our faith and nudging us to rely on our own reasoning, often at the expense of our belief. Rooted in uncertainty, doubt breeds confusion and can lead us astray. Although it is common to experience doubt, we must remember that God is not a source of confusion (1 Corinthians 14:33, ESV). He does not instill doubt where He has already provided assurance in His Word. Without the discernment to recognize truth, we risk overlooking God's presence and work in our lives.

Many of us may navigate life unaware of our doubts. However, turning to God in prayer can heighten our awareness of these uncertainties. Frequently, God is actively addressing our doubts long before we recognize the need for guidance. He knows our hearts intimately (Luke 16:15, NIV) and is fully aware of our struggles with doubt, irrespective of our self-perceptions.

{ **By bringing our doubts before God, we open ourselves to deeper truths and reinforce the understanding that faith is essential for cultivating a hopeful existence.** }

God can deliver us from hardship and genuinely cares about our circumstances. His ways are ordered and purposeful, opposing any doubt threatening to undermine our faith. Ultimately, overcoming doubt through faith is one of the most transformative steps we can take toward a renewed and enriched life.

PETITION:

Lord, take away any spirit of doubt and help me recognize Your handiwork throughout my life. Grant me a pure and undivided heart that approaches You in awe of Your power and majesty. Keep me from seeking to quench my spiritual thirst with broken cisterns, and help me continually draw from the wellspring of Living Water that is You. May I use Your Word as my guiding light and persevere in truth. Guide me to my purpose and the life You have created for me.

GRATITUDE:

I am grateful I don't have to see to believe. I am grateful I can feel Your presence and seek You through prayer and reading your Word. You have provided purpose for my life and I am grateful I can use it for Your glory.

INTERCESSION:

I pray that others may overcome any unbelief and doubt. May they seek Your provision as they turn to You in times of uncertainty, believing in good things as they view life through the lens of faith. I pray they will earnestly seek Your will in all they do and trust You with their decisions and future.

AMEN

Mark 11:22-24; Hebrews 11:6; Romans 10:17

CONCLUSION
Remaining in the Father's House

As we come to the end of this devotional, I pray you feel encouraged, strengthened, and closer to the God who never leaves or forsakes us. These past thirty days were not just about reflection, but about stepping into the truth of who God is and who He created you to be. Healing, growth, and transformation are not always quick or easy, but they are always possible when we remain rooted in His love and guided by His Word.

If you take away anything from this journey, let it be this: You are not defined by your struggles or your past. You are defined by the love of a Savior who calls you His own. Like the prodigal, no matter how far you have wandered or how heavy your burdens have been, God welcomes you with open arms. He does not meet you with shame or condemnation, but with grace, forgiveness, and the promise of new beginnings.

As you move forward, keep practicing the habits you have built over these thirty days. Continue to pour your heart out in prayer, find joy in gratitude, and pray earnestly for others. These simple acts will keep you connected to God and grounded in His peace. Remember, your journey does not end here; this is only the beginning. God has a purpose for your life, and the work He is doing in you will ripple out to bless others in ways you may never see.

Take heart in knowing that God's faithfulness is unchanging. His mercies are new every morning, and His plans for you are good. Whatever challenges or victories lie ahead, you can face them with confidence because He is with you. Step boldly into the future, trusting that the God who brought you this far will continue to guide you every step of the way.

You are loved, you are chosen, and you are never alone. Hold on to the truth of His Word, and remember that every step you take toward Him brings you closer to the life of freedom and joy He has designed for you. Keep going, keep trusting, and always remember—*you are home in Him.*

ACKNOWLEDGEMENTS

All glory to God. Since I gave my life to Christ, my life has radically transformed, and I pray I will always steward well everything I have been given.

I want to express my deepest gratitude to my husband, Sam. You are the love of my life and my best friend. Thank you for always supporting my dreams and being my steadfast companion. You are my rock, my safe place, and my favorite person. The way you father our girls is inspiring, and I cannot imagine doing this life with anyone else. Thank you for leading our family so well.

To my four beautiful daughters: Salia, Kya, Fae, and Lovai— my life is overflowing because of you. You are the greatest gifts, and I am so proud of the remarkable individuals you are becoming. Always remember that your identity is in Christ, and in Him alone.

To my Nanny: I pray to have faith like yours. One of my biggest regrets is being wayward toward the end of your life. You left an indelible mark on my faith, and I know it was your prayers that guided me back home.

To my Mom: I love you dearly. I have watched you navigate life with such grace, embodying what it means to be meek and a strong woman of faith. Thank you for always believing in me.

To my dear sisters in Christ: Your joy in Jesus is truly contagious. You are among the most gifted women I know, and you've been there for me in my moments of greatest need. Your guidance and encouraging words have been a lifeline. I can't imagine life without you all!

To my mentor, Miranda: I look up to you in countless ways. Thank you for always believing in me and serving as a sounding board. I aspire to lead with the same grace you do. Your ability to make people feel seen and understood is a rare gift, and I wouldn't be where I am without your love and encouragement.

To all of my Bible study girls: Thank you for walking alongside me and for your unwavering prayers. You have been with me from the beginning, and I am blessed to have such a faithful community. I pray we will always be the salt and light of the earth. How blessed we are to know Jesus! May we spread the Good News to the ends of the earth.

RESOURCES
Faith-Based Resources

1. **Celebrate Recovery**
   A Christ-centered recovery program for anyone struggling with hurt, pain, or addiction.
   Website: celebraterecovery.com

2. **The Salvation Army Adult Rehabilitation Centers**
   Faith-based recovery programs that provide residential treatment and spiritual guidance.
   Website: salvationarmyusa.org

3. **Focus on the Family's Counseling Services**
   Offers Christian-based counseling and referrals to trusted therapists.
   Website: focusonthefamily.com

4. **Pure Desire Ministries**
   Specializes in recovery for those struggling with sexual addiction or other compulsive behaviors.
   Website: puredesire.org

National Addiction Resources

1. **Substance Abuse and Mental Health Services Administration (SAMHSA)**
   Offers a national helpline (1-800-662-HELP) for treatment referrals and crisis support.
   Website: samhsa.gov

2. **Shatterproof**
   A nonprofit organization providing addiction resources and treatment locators.
   Website: shatterproof.org

3. **Alcoholics Anonymous (AA) and Narcotics Anonymous (NA)**
   Peer-led support groups for those recovering from alcohol and drug addiction.
   Website (AA): aa.org
   Website (NA): na.org

Mental Health Support

1. **National Alliance on Mental Illness (NAMI)**
   Provides education, advocacy, and support for those living with mental health conditions.
   Helpline: 1-800-950-NAMI
   Website: nami.org

2. **Crisis Text Line**
   Free, 24/7 support for anyone in crisis. Text HOME to 741741 to connect with a trained counselor.
   Website: crisistextline.org

3. **BetterHelp or Faithful Counseling**
   Online platforms that connect individuals with licensed counselors, including faith-based options.
   Website (BetterHelp): betterhelp.com
   Website (Faithful Counseling): faithfulcounseling.com

Bible

1. **"The Life Recovery Bible" (Tyndale House Publishers)**
   A Bible specifically designed for those in recovery, with devotionals and practical steps.

ABOUT THE AUTHOR

Jaana Woodbury is a passionate speaker, author, and advocacy leader whose life was radically transformed after overcoming addiction and encountering the grace of God. Now a devoted wife and mother of four, her story has been shared on national platforms, including the Emmy Award–winning Sesame Street series Parental Addiction, and through partnerships with organizations like Shatterproof and Tennessee's "You Are Not Alone" campaign.

She writes for the YouVersion Bible App and has released three devotionals, including one that reached over 252 countries and saw more than 40,000 completions in under 60 days. Jaana also serves on the Junior Board for Shatterproof, a national nonprofit dedicated to ending the addiction crisis in the United States and shares gospel-centered content that points people to the truth found in Christ—reaching the lost, encouraging believers, and equipping Bible study enthusiasts through her passion for Scripture and her growing online community, including on the YouVersion Bible App.

She is currently pursuing her theological studies at Dallas Theological Seminary and lives in College Grove, TN, with her husband Sam, their four daughters, and their two German Shepherds, Gideon and Asher. She loves slow mornings, open Bibles, and watching people come alive to the call of God on their lives. You can learn more at www.jaanawoodbury.com or follow along on Instagram @jaanawoodbury.

www.ingramcontent.com/pod-product-compliance
Lightning Source LLC
Chambersburg PA
CBHW040252090526
44586CB00041B/2786